Dance And The Soul

Dance And The Soul

Paul Valéry

Translated by
Will Johncock

Planktos Press

Published by Planktos Press.
Sydney, Australia.
www.planktospress.com

Copyright © 2023

All rights reserved. Except for brief quotations in critical publications or reviews, no part of this book may be reproduced in any manner without prior permission from the publisher.

Paperback ISBN: 978-1-922931-03-0
Hardback ISBN: 978-1-922931-04-7
eBook ISBN: 978-1-922931-05-4

Dance And The Soul was originally published in French under the title *L'Âme et la Danse (1921)*, by Librairie Gallimard, Paris.

Eryximachus

Oh Socrates, I die!... Give me spirit! Pour me ideas!... Bring to my nostrils your acute enigmas!... This pitiless meal exceeds all conceivable appetite and all believable thirst!... What a state, to succeed to good things, and to inherit a digestion!... My soul is no longer anything but a dream of matter in conflict with itself!... Oh good things and too good things, I arrange for you to pass!... Alas, since as day fell we have been plagued by what is best in the world, this terrible best, multiplied by duration, imposes its unbearable presence... And now I perish from a crazy longing for things that are dry, and serious, and quite spiritual!... Permit me to come sit beside you and Phaedrus ; my back deliberately turned upon those perpetually recurring meats and those inexhaustible urns, let me hold out to your words the supreme cup of my spirit. What were you saying?

Phaedrus

Nothing, yet. We were watching our

fellows eat and drink…

Eryximachus

But Socrates must have been meditating about something?... Can he ever remain solitary with himself, and silent in his very soul! He was tenderly smiling at his demon, on the mysterious edges of this feast. What are your lips murmuring, dear Socrates?

Socrates

They say to me gently : the man who eats is the most just of men…

Eryximachus

Here is the enigma already, and the appetite of the spirit which it is made to arouse…

Socrates

The man who eats, say my lips, feeds his own goods and ills. Each mouthful which he feels melt and dissipate within himself, brings new strength to his virtues, as it does indiscriminately to his vices. It sustains his torments just as it fattens his hopes ; and is divided somewhere between passions and reasons. Love needs it as does hate ; and my joy and my bitterness, my memory and my projects, share like brothers the very substance of one and the same mouthful. What do you think, son of Acumenus?

Eryximachus

I think that I think as you do.

Socrates

Oh doctor that you are, I was silently admiring the acts of all these feeding bodies. Each one, without knowledge, gives fairly what comes to them to each chance of life, to each germ of death, within itself. They do not know what they are doing, but they do it like gods do.

Eryximachus

I have long observed it : all that enters into

man very soon behaves as the Fates please. One would say that it is as if the isthmus of the throat is the threshold of capricious necessities and organized mystery. There, ceases the will, and the certain empire of knowledge. That is why I have renounced, in the practice of my art, all those fickle drugs which ordinary doctors impose on the range of their ill patients ; and I keep strictly to obvious remedies, compounded one part for another by their nature.

Phaedrus

What remedies?

Eryximachus

There are eight : heat, cold ; abstinence and its contrary ; air and water ; rest and movement. That is all.

Socrates

But for the soul there are only two, Eryximachus.

Phaedrus

Which ones are they?

Socrates

Truth and falsehood.

Phaedrus

How is that?

Socrates

Are they not to one another as waking is to sleeping? Do you not seek awakening and the clarity of light when a bad dream gets to you? Are we not resuscitated by the sun in person, and fortified by the presence of solid bodies? – But, on the other hand, is it not true that we ask sleep and dreams to dissolve our worries and to suspend the troubles which sit astride us in the world of day? And so, we flee from one into the other, invoking day in the middle of the night ; imploring, on the contrary, darkness whilst we have light ; anxious to know, yet too happy to ignore, we seek in what is, a remedy for what is not ; and in what is not, a relief for what is. Sometimes the real, sometimes the illusion on which we meditate ; and the soul, definitively, has no other resource than the true, which is her weapon – and falsehood, her armour.

Eryximachus

Good, good... But do you not fear, dear Socrates, a certain consequence from that thought which has come to you?

Socrates

What consequence?

Eryximachus

This one : that truth and falsehood tend to the same end... It is one and the same thing, which, in going about in various ways, makes us liars or truthful ; and like sometimes the heat, and sometimes the cold, sometimes attack us, sometimes defend us, so the true and the false, and the opposing wills that relate to them.

Socrates

Nothing is more certain. I cannot do anything about it. It is life itself which wants it : you know better than I, that it makes use of everything. Everything is good for it, Eryximachus, in order that it never concludes. It is therefore that it only concludes as itself… Is it not this mysterious movement which, by the detour of everything that happens, incessantly transforms me into myself, and which brings me back quickly enough to this same Socrates so that I find him again, and that in imagining myself necessarily to recognise him, I am! – Life is a woman who dances, and who would cease divinely to be a woman, if the leap that she has made, she was able to obey to the skies. But as we can go to infinity, neither in dream nor in wakefulness, she, likewise, always becomes herself again ; ceases to be a snowflake, bird, idea ; ceases to be finally all that it pleased the flute that she was, because the same Earth which sent her, calls her back, and returns her breathless to her woman's nature and to her friend...

Phaedrus

A miracle!... Marvellous man!... Almost a true miracle! As soon as you speak, you generate what is necessary!... Your images cannot remain images!... Here it is precisely, – as if from your creative mouth, was born the bee, and the bee, and the bee, – here is the winged choir of the illustrious dancers!... The air hums and buzzes with the omens of the orchestra!... All the torches awaken... The murmur of the sleepers is transformed ; and on the walls of agitated flames, the huge shadows of drunkards marvel and worry... See this half-light, half-solemn troop! – They enter like souls!

Socrates

By the gods, the bright dancers!... What a lively and graceful introduction of the most perfect thoughts!... Their hands speak, and their feet seem to write. What precision in these beings who study in order to use their tender strengths so felicitously!... All my difficulties desert me, and there is now no problem that exerts me, so much do I happily obey the mobility of those figures! Here, certainty is a game ; it seems that knowledge has found its act, and that intelligence suddenly consents to spontaneous graces... See this one, this dancer!... The slimmest and the most absorbed in pure rightness... Who is she?... She is deliciously hard, and inexpressibly supple... She yields, she borrows, she returns the cadence so exactly, that if I shut my eyes, I see her exactly by hearing. I follow her, and I find her again, and I can never lose her ; and if, my ears blocked, I look at her, so much is she rhythm and music, that it is impossible for me to not hear the zithers.

Phaedrus

It is Rhodopis, I believe, that is the one who delights you.

Socrates

For Rhodopis, then, the ear is wonderfully linked to the ankle... How right she is!... Old time is all rejuvenated!

Eryximachus

But no, Phaedrus!... Rhodopis is the other, so gentle, and so easy for the eye to caress indefinitely.

Socrates

But who then is the slender monster of suppleness?

Eryximachus

Rhodonia.

Socrates

For Rhodonia, then, the ear is wonderfully linked to the ankle.

Eryximachus

Moreover, I know them all, and each

individually. I can tell you all their names. They can be arranged very well into a small poem that is remembered easily : Nips, Nephoë, Nema – Nikteris, Nephele, Nexis – Rhodopis, Rhodonia, Ptile... As for the little dancer who is so ugly, they name him Nettarion... But the queen of the choir has not yet entered.

Phaedrus

And who rules over these bees?

Eryximachus

The astonishing and extreme dancer, Athikte!

Phaedrus

How well you know them!

Eryximachus

All this charming company have lots of other names! Some come to them from their parents ; and the others, from their intimate partners...

Phaedrus

That is you, the intimate one!... You know them much too well!

Eryximachus

I know them much better than well, and in some way, a little better than they know themselves. Oh Phaedrus, am I not the doctor – In me, through me, all the secrets of medicine are secretly exchanged for all the secrets of the dancer! They call me for everything. Sprains, pimples, fantasies, heartaches, the various accidents of their profession (and those substantial accidents which easily derive from a very mobile career), – and their mysterious ailments ; indeed even jealousy, whether artistic or passionate ; even dreams!... Do you know that they only have to whisper to me about some dream which torments them, for me to conclude, for example, the deterioration of some tooth?

Socrates

Admirable man, who through dreams knows teeth, do you think that philosophers have theirs all ruined?

Eryximachus

Gods, preserve me from the bit of Socrates!

Phaedrus

Look instead at these innumerable arms and legs!... Some women do a thousand things. A thousand torches, a thousand ephemeral peristyles, climbing vines, columns... The images melt into each other, disappear... It is a grove of beautiful branches all agitated by the breezes of the music! Is it a dream, Eryximachus, that signifies more torments, and more dangerous corruptions of our minds?

Socrates

But this is precisely the opposite of a dream, dear Phaedrus.

Phaedrus

But *I* dream... I dream of the softness, multiplying indefinitely through itself, of these encounters, and of these exchanges of virgin forms. I dream of those inexpressible contacts which occur in the soul, between the beats, between the whitenesses and the passes of those members in measure, and the accents of that muffled sound on which all things seem painted and carried... I breathe, like a musky and compounded smell, this mix of charming girls ; and my presence gets lost in this maze of graces, where each dancer loses herself with a companion, and finds herself with another.

Socrates

Voluptuous soul, see therefore here the opposite of a dream, and the absent coincidence... But what is the opposite of a dream, Phaedrus, if not some other dream?... A dream of vigilance and of tension that would make Reason itself! – And what would such a Reason dream? –

If such a Reason dreamed, hard, standing, eye armed, mouth closed, like a mistress of her lips, – would the dream that she had not be what we see now, – this world of exact forces and studied illusions? – A dream, a dream, but a dream penetrated of all symmetries, all order, all acts and sequences!... Who knows what noble Laws dream here that they have taken clear features, and that they accord in the purpose of manifesting to the mortals how the real, the unreal, and the intelligible can merge and combine according to the power of the Muses?

Eryximachus

It is quite true, Socrates, that the treasure of these images is invaluable... Do you not think that the thought of the Immortals is precisely what we see, and that the infinity of these noble similarities, conversions, inversions, inexhaustible diversions which answer and deduce themselves before our eyes, transport us into the divine knowledge?

Phaedrus

How pure it is, how graceful, this small, pink and round temple that they form now, and which turns as slowly as the night!... It clears into young girls, the tunics fly away, and the gods seem to change their mind!...

Eryximachus

The divine thought is at present this multicoloured abundance of groups of smiling figures ; it generates the repetitions of these delightful manoeuvres, these voluptuous whirls which form from two or three bodies and which can no longer be broken... One of the dancers is like a captive. She will no longer leave their enchanted chains!...

Socrates

But what are they doing all of a sudden?... They get tangled up confusedly, they run away!...

Phaedrus

They fly to the doors. They bow to welcome.

Eryximachus

Athikte! Athikte! Oh gods!... The thrilling Athikte!

Socrates

She is nothing.

Phaedrus

Little bird!

Socrates

A thing without a body!

Eryximachus

A thing without a price!

Phaedrus

Oh Socrates, it seems as if she was obeying invisible figures!

Socrates

Or that she yields to some noble destiny!

Eryximachus

Look! Look!... She begins, do you see? With a walk all divine : it is a simple, circular walk... She begins with her art at its most supreme ; she walks naturally on the summit that she has reached. This second nature is the furthest from the first, but it is necessary that they be alike so that they are mistaken for each other.

Socrates

I enjoy this magnificent freedom like no one else. The others, now, are set in place and as though they are enchanted. The musicians listen to themselves, whilst not losing sight of her... They adhere to their role and seem to insist on the perfection of their accompaniment.

Phaedrus

One, of pink coral, and curiously bent,

blows in an enormous shell.

Eryximachus

The very tall flutist with slender thighs, tightly woven together, stretches out her elegant foot whose toe marks the beat... Oh Socrates, what do you think of the dancer?

Socrates

Eryximachus, this little being makes you think… It gathers to itself, it assumes a majesty which was confused in all of us, and which imperceptibly inhabited the actors of this debauchery… A simple walk, and goddess, here she is ; and we, almost gods!... A simple walk, the simplest sequence!... It is as though she pays for the space with beautiful and equal acts, and that she hits with her heel, the resonant effigies of the movement. She seems to list and count in pure gold coins, what we distractedly spend in a common currency of steps, when we walk to any purpose.

Eryximachus

Dear Socrates, she teaches us what we do, showing clearly to our souls, what our bodies accomplish obscurely. In the light of her legs, our immediate movements appear to us as miracles. They surprise us, finally, as much as they should.

Phaedrus

In what way would this dancer have, according to you, something Socratic, teaching us, in regard to walking, to know ourselves a little better?

Eryximachus

Clearly. Our steps are so easy and familiar to us that they never have the honour of being considered in themselves, and as strange acts (unless if disabled or cripped, the deprivation of steps leads us to admire them)… They lead therefore as they know, we who naively ignore them ; and according to the terrain, the goal, the mood, the state of man, or even the illuminance of the way, they are what they are : we lose them without thinking about them.

But consider this perfect procession of Athikte, over the faultless floor, free, definite, and hardly elastic. She places with symmetry on this mirror of her forces, her alternating supports ; her heel pouring the body towards the toe, the other foot passing and receiving the body, and pouring it forwards again ; and so on, and so on ; whilst the adorable top of her head traces in the eternal present, the forehead of an undulating wave.

As the ground here is in a way absolute, being carefully freed from all causes of uncertainty and a lack of rhythm, this monumental march which has only itself for a goal, and from which all variable impurities have disappeared, becomes a universal model.

See what beauty, what full security of the

soul results from this length of her noble strides. This amplitude of her steps accords with their number, which emanates directly from the music. But number and length are, on the other hand, secretly in harmony with height…

Socrates

You speak so well about these things, learned Eryximachus, that I cannot help myself from seeing according to your thought. I contemplate this woman who walks and yet gives me the feeling of stillness. I concern myself only with the equality of these measures…

Phaedrus

She stops, in the middle of these commensurable graces…

Eryximachus

You will see!

Phaedrus

She shuts her eyes…

Socrates

She is entirely in her closed eyes, and all alone with her soul, in the heart of intimate attention… She feels in herself she is becoming some event.

Eryximachus

Wait for… Silence, silence!

Phaedrus

Delicious moment… This silence is contradiction... How can on not shout out : Silence!

Socrates

Absolutely virginal moment. And then, the moment when something must break in the soul, in wait, in expectation, in the assembly… Something breaks… And yet, it is also like a welding.

Eryximachus

Athikte! How excellent you are in imminence!

Phaedrus

Music seems to gently seize her again in another way, lifts her up…

Eryximachus

Music changes her soul.

Socrates

You are, oh Muses, in this moment that is going to die, all-powerful mistresses!

Delicious suspense of breaths and hearts!… Gravity falls at her feet ; and this great veil that comes crashing down without any noise makes it clear. Her body must only be seen in movement.

Eryximachus

Her eyes have returned to the light…

Phaedrus

Let us enjoy the very delicate moment when she changes her will!... Like the bird that arrived at the very edge of the roof, breaks with the beautiful marble, and falls into its flight…

Eryximachus

I love nothing as much as that which is going to happen ; and even in love, I find nothing that surpasses in sensual pleasure the very first feelings. Of all the hours of the day, dawn is my favourite. That is why I want to see with a tender emotion, the sacred movement, dawning on this living creature. See!... It is born from this sliding glance which invincibly leads the head with the soft nostrils towards the well-lit shoulder… And the whole beautiful fibre of her clean and muscular body, from the neck to the heel, progressively expresses and twists itself ; and the whole thing shudders… She slowly draws a leap about to be born… She forbids us to breathe until the moment that she springs, responding with a sudden act to the expected and yet unexpected clap of the ripping cymbals!...

Socrates

Oh! So here she is finally, entering the exception and penetrating what it is not possible to penetrate!... How similar our souls are, oh my friends, before this prestige, which is equal and complete, for each of them!... How they drink together what is beautiful!

Eryximachus

All of her becomes dance, and wholly dedicated to total movement!

Phaedrus

She seems at first, from her steps full of spirit, to erase from the earth all fatigue, and all foolishness... And here it is, she makes herself a residence a little above things, as though she is sorting out a nest for herself in her white arms... But, now, do you not believe that she weaves from her feet an indefinable carpet of sensations?... She crosses, she uncrosses, she hatches the world with time... Oh what charming work, the very precious labour of her intelligent toes which attack, which dodge, which knot and unknot, which chase each other, which fly away!... How skilful they are, how lively, these pure crafters of the delights of lost time!... These two feet babble between themselves, and quarrel like doves!... The same spot on the ground makes them fight as if for a grain!... They fly into a rage together, and clash each other again in the air!... By the Muses, never have feet made my lips more envious!

Socrates

Here therefore your lips are envious of the confident and eloquent speech of these prodigious feet! You would like to feel their wings in your words, and to adorn what you say with figures as lively as their leaps!

Phaedrus

Me?...

Eryximachus

He was only thinking about kissing those feet, those turtledoves!... It is an effect of this passionate attention that he gives to the spectacle of the dance. What could be more natural, Socrates, what could be more ingeniously mysterious?... Our Phaedrus is very dazzled with these points, and with these sparkling pirouettes, which mark the fair pride of the tips of Athikte's toes ; he devours them with his eyes, he stretches his face to them ; he believes he can feel the agile onyx running on his lips! – Do not apologise, dear Phaedrus, do not be the least bit confused!... You have felt nothing that is not legitimate and obscure, and therefore, conforming perfectly with the mortal machine. Are we not an organised fantasy? Is our living system not a functioning incoherence, and a disorder which acts? – Do not events, desires, ideas, interchange within us in the most necessary and incomprehensible way?... What a cacophony of causes and effects!...

Phaedrus

You have explained very well what I have innocently felt…

Socrates

Dear Phaedrus, in truth, you were not moved without some reason. The more I look at this inexpressible dancer, the more I talk to myself about wonders. I worry how nature knew how to enclose in this girl so frail and fine, such a monster of strength and swiftness. Hercules changed into a swallow – does this myth exist? And how does this head, as little and tight as a young pine cone, unerringly generate these myriad questions and answers amongst its limbs, and these dizzying gropings that it produces and reproduces, incessantly repudiating them, receiving them from the music and immediately returning them to the light.

Eryximachus

And I, for my part, think of the power of the insect, whose innumerable vibrations of its wings indefinitely support the fanfare, weight, and courage!...

Socrates

This one struggles in the web of our looks, like a captured fly. But my curious mind runs on the web after her, and wants to devour what she accomplishes!

Phaedrus

Dear Socrates, can you only ever enjoy yourself?

Socrates

Oh my friends, what really is dance?

Eryximachus

Is it not what we see? – What do you want to be clearer about dance, than the dance itself?

Phaedrus

Our Socrates only stops when he has grasped the soul of everything : if not, even, the soul of the soul!

Socrates

But what then is dance, and what can steps say?

Phaedrus

Oh! Let's enjoy a little more, naively, of these beautiful acts... To the right, to the left ; forward, backward, upward and downward, she seems to offer some gifts, perfumes, incense, kisses, and her life itself, to all points of the sphere, and to the poles of the universe…

She traces dews, intertwinings, stars of movement, and magical enclosures… She leaps out of barely closed circles… She leaps and runs after phantoms!... She picks a flower, which is immediately a smile!... Oh! How she proclaims her non-existence by an inexhaustible lightness!... She goes astray in the midst of the sounds, she recovers herself by a thread... It is the helpful flute that saved her! Oh melody!...

Socrates

It seems now that everything around her is only spectres... She gives birth to them whilst fleeing them ; but if, suddenly, she turns around, it seems to us that she appears to the immortals!...

Phaedrus

Is she not the soul of fables, and the breakaway from all the doors of life?

Eryximachus

Do you believe she knows anything about it? And that she flatters herself about producing other prodigies than high kicks, beats, and leaps learned with difficulty during her apprenticeship?

Socrates

It is true that one can also unquestionably consider things under this light... A cold eye would easily look at her as crazy, this strangely uprooted woman, who incessantly tears herself away from her own form, whilst her limbs, having become mad, seem to fight for the earth and air ; and her head thrown back, drags a loose hair on the ground ; and one of her legs is in place of that head ; and her finger traces signs I do not know in the dust!... After all, why all this? It is enough that the soul remains stationary and refuses itself, for it to conceive only the strangeness and disgust of this ridiculous agitation... If you want it, my soul, all this is absurd.

Eryximachus

You can therefore, depending on your mood, understand, not understand ; find beautiful, find ridiculous, as you wish?

Socrates

It is necessary that it is so…

Phaedrus

Do you mean, dear Socrates, that your reason considers dance a stranger, whose language it scorns, and whose behaviours seem inexplicable to it, if not shocking ; if not even entirely obscene?

Eryximachus

Reason, sometimes, seems to me to be the faculty of our soul that understands nothing about our body!

Phaedrus

But me, Socrates, contemplating the dancer makes me think of many things, and of many relationships between things, which, immediately, become my own thought, and think, as it were, in Phaedrus' place. I find clarity that I never would have obtained from the presence of my soul alone…

Just now, for example, Athikte seemed to me to represent love – Which love? – Not this one, nor that one ; and not some miserable affair! Certainly, she was not playing the role of a lover… No mime, no theatre! No, no! No fiction! Why feign, my friends, when movement and measurement are available to us, which are what is real in the real?... She was therefore the very being of love! But what is it, love? Of what is it made? How to define and paint it? We know well that the soul of love is the invincible difference between lovers, whilst its subtle matter is the identity of their desires. Dance must therefore give birth to subtle features, by the divinity of its style and vigour, by the delicacy of its stationary tiptoes, this universal creature which has neither body nor face, but which has gifts, days, and destinies, but which has a life and a death ; and which is even only life and death, because desire, once born, knows neither sleep nor respite.

This is why only the dancer can make love

visible through her beautiful acts. All of her, Socrates, all of her was love!... She was games and tears, and useless feints! Charms, falls, offerings ; and surprises and yeses, and noes, and sadly lost steps... She celebrated all the mysteries of absence and presence ; she seemed sometimes to brush against ineffable catastrophes!... But now, to give thanks to Aphrodite, look at her. Is she not suddenly a veritable wave of the sea? Now heavier than her body, now lighter than her body, she leaps, as if sprayed from a rock ; she drops softly... She is a wave!

Eryximachus

Phaedrus, at all costs, claims that she represents something!

Phaedrus

What do you think, Socrates!

Socrates

Whether she represents anything at all?

Phaedrus

Yes. Do you think that she represents something?

Socrates

Nothing, dear Phaedrus. But everything, Eryximachus. Love, as well as the sea, and life itself, and thoughts… Do you not feel that she is the pure act of metamorphosis?

Phaedrus

Divine Socrates, you know what simple and singular confidence I have placed, since I have known you, in your incomparable lights : I cannot hear you without believing you, nor believe you without enjoying myself believing you. But I find it almost unbearable to hear that Athikte's dancing represents nothing, and is not, above all things, an image of the outbursts and graces of love…

Socrates

I have not said anything so cruel yet! Oh

my friends, I am only asking what dance is ; and each of you respectively appears to know ; but to know it quite separately! One of you tells me that it is what it is, and that it is reduced to what our eyes see here ; and the other holds very firmly that it represents something, and therefore that it is not entirely in itself, but principally in us. As for me, my friends, my uncertainty is intact!... My thoughts are numerous, which never is a good sign!... Numerous, confused, evenly crowded around me...

Eryximachus

You complain about being rich!

Socrates

Opulence makes you immobile. But my desire is movement, Eryximachus... What I need now is the delicate power that is the hallmark of the bee, as it is the sovereign good of the dancer... My mind would need this force and concentrated movement, which suspend the insect above the multitude of flowers ; which make it the vibrant arbiter of the diversity of their corollas ; which present it as it pleases to this or that flower, to that rose a little further away ; and which allow it to touch it, to flee from it, or to penetrate it… These forces suddenly take it away from the flower it has finishing loving, just as soon as they bring it back to that flower, if it repents for having left something sweet in it the memory of which follows it, and the sweetness of which haunts it for the rest of its flight… Or would I need, oh Phaedrus, the subtle displacement of the dancer, which, creeping into my thoughts, would delicately awaken each of them in turn, bringing them out from under the shadow of my soul, and appear in the light of your minds, in the happiest of all possible orders.

Phaedrus

Speak, speak… I see the bee on your lips, and the dancer in your look.

Eryximachus

Speak, oh master of the divine art of trusting the budding idea!... The ever-fortunate author of the wonderful consequences of a dialectical accident!... Speak! Pull the golden thread... Bring from your deep absences some living truth!

Phaedrus

Chance is on your side... It changes imperceptibly into wisdom, as you chase it with your voice in the labyrinth of your soul!

Socrates

Well, first of all, I would like to consult our doctor!

Eryximachus

Whatever you like, dear Socrates.

Socrates

Tell me then, son of Acumenus, oh Therapeut Eryximachus, you for whom bitter drugs and dark spices have so few hidden virtues that you make no use of them ; you then, who possessing as well as any man of the world, all the secrets of art and those of nature, yet do not prescribe, nor advocate, balms, bowls, or mysterious fillers ; you, you, of all people, who does not trust elixirs, who does not believe in anonymous potions ; oh healer without palatable medicines, disdainful of all that – powders, drops, gums, lumps, flakes, gems or crystals – snatches the tongue, pierces the olfactory vaults, touches the springs of sneezing or nausea, kills or invigorates ; tell me then, dear friend Eryximachus, of the healers the most knowledgeable in medical substances, tell me this : do you not know, amongst so many active and efficient substances, and amongst those masterly preparations that your science contemplates as vain or detestable weapons in the arsenal of the pharmacopoeia, – tell me then, do you not know some specific remedy, or any exact antidote, for that evil of all evils, that poison of poisons, that venom opposed to all of nature?...

Phaedrus

What venom?

Socrates

… That which is called : the weariness of living – I mean, please know, not temporary weariness ; not weariness by fatigue, or weariness of which we see the germ, or know the limits ; but that perfect weariness, that pure weariness, that weariness which is not caused by misfortune, weakness or ailment, and which is compatible with the happiest of all contemplatable conditions – that weariness, which has no other substance than life itself, and no other second cause than the clear-sightedness of the living. This absolute weariness is in itself nothing except the nakedness of life, when it looks at itself clearly.

Eryximachus

It is true that if our soul purges itself of all falsehoods, and deprives itself of every fraudulent addition to what is, our existence is immediately threatened, by this cold, exact, reasonable and moderate consideration of human life as it is.

Phaedrus

Life darkens on contact with truth, just as the dubious mushroom does when crushed on contact with the air.

Socrates

Eryximachus, I was asking you if there was a cure?

Eryximachus

Why cure such a rational ailment? Nothing, without doubt, is more morbid in itself, nothing is more hostile to nature, than to see things as they are. A cold and perfect clarity is a poison that is impossible to fight. The real, in its pure state, instantly stops the heart... One drop of that icy lymph suffices to relax in a soul the springs and palpitations of desire, exterminate all hopes, ruin all the gods who were in our blood. The Virtues and the most noble colours are paled by it, and devoured little by little. The past, reduced to a few ashes by it ; the future, to a small icicle. The soul appears to itself as an empty and measurable form. Here, then, are things as they are that come together, which limit one another, and are chained together in the most rigorous and mortal way... Oh Socrates, the universe cannot endure, for a single moment, to be only what it is. It is strange to think that which is the Whole cannot be self-sufficient... Its dread at being what is, has therefore made it create and paint a thousand masks ; there is no other reason for the existence of mortals. For what are mortals? Their business is to know. Know? And what does it mean to know? It is certainly not to be what one is. So here are humans delirious and thinking, introducing into nature the principle of unlimited errors, and this myriad of marvels!...

The mistakes, the appearances, the play of refractions of the mind, deepen and enliven the miserable mass of the world... The idea introduces into what is, the leaven of what is not… But the truth sometimes at last breaks out, and stands out in the harmonious system of phantasmagoria and errors… Everything immediately threatens to perish, and Socrates himself comes to me to request a remedy for this desperate case of clear-sightedness and weariness!...

Socrates

Well, Eryximachus, as there is no cure, can you at least tell me, which state is most opposite to that horrible state of pure disgust, of deadly lucidity, and of unmoved clarity?

Eryximachus

First I see all the non-melancholic delusions.

Socrates

And then?

Eryximachus

Drunkenness, and the category of illusions caused by heady vapours.

Socrates

Yes. But are there not intoxications which do not have their source in wine?

Eryximachus

Certainly. Love, hate, greed, each intoxicate!... And the feeling of power...

Socrates

All this gives taste and colour to life. But the chance of hating, or of loving, or of acquiring very great possessions, is linked to all the hazards of reality... Do you not see then, Eryximachus, that amongst all the intoxications, the most noble, and the most hostile to great weariness, is intoxication due to actions? Our acts, and particularly those of our actions which set our bodies in motion, can bring us into a strange and admirable stage… It is the state the furthest removed from this sad state in which we left the motionless and lucid observer that we imagined earlier.

Phaedrus

But what if, by some miracle, this observer was taken by a sudden passion for dance?… If he wanted to stop being clear in order to become light ; and if then, trying to differentiate himself infinitely from himself, he tried to change his freedom of judgement into freedom of movement?

Socrates

In such circumstances he would teach us at once what we are trying to elucidate now… But I still have something that I need to ask Eryximachus.

Eryximachus

Whatever you want, dear Socrates.

Socrates

Tell me then, wise physician, who in your travels and studies has deepened your knowledge of all living things ; the great connoisseur that you are of natural forms and whims, you who has distinguished yourself in the classification of remarkable animals and plants (the harmful and the benign ; the harmless and the effective ; the surprising, awful, the ridiculous ; the dubious ; and finally, those that do not exist), – tell me then, have you not heard of those strange animals that live and thrive in the flame itself?

Eryximachus

Certainly!... Their faces and habits, dear Socrates, have been well studied ; although their very existence has recently been the subject of some dispute. I have very often described them to my disciples ; however I have never had the chance to see them for myself.

Socrates

Well then, does it not seem to you, Eryximachus, and to you, my dear Phaedrus, that this creature which stirs over there, fidgeting adorably in our gaze, this ardent Athikte who divides and gathers herself together again, who rises and falls, opens and closes so quickly, and who appears to belong to constellations other than ours – looks alive, completely at ease, in an element comparable to fire – in a very subtle essence of music and movement, where she breathes inexhaustible energy, whilst she participates with all her being in the pure and immediate violence of extreme bliss? – What if we compare our weighty and serious condition with this state of this sparkling salamander, does it not seem that our ordinary acts, generated successively by our needs, our gestures and accidental movements, are like coarse materials, like an impure matter of duration – whilst this exaltation and vibration of life, this supremacy of tension, and this rapture in being the most agile that one can be, have the virtues and powers of flame ; and that the shames, the worries, the sillinesses, and the monotonous sustenance of existence are consumed in it, making what is divine in a mortal woman shine in our eyes?

Phaedrus

Admirable Socrates, look quickly, how truthfully you speak!... Look at the thrilling one! You would think that dance bursts out of her body like a flame!

Socrates

Oh Flame!...
– Perhaps this girl is a fool?... Oh Flame!...
– And who knows what superstitions and nonsense make up her ordinary soul?

Oh Flame, nevertheless!... Lively and divine thing!...

But what is a flame, oh my friends, if not *the moment itself?* – What is crazy, and joyful joyous and formidable in the very moment?... Flame is the act of that moment which is between the earth and heaven. Oh my friends, everything that passes from the heavy state to the subtle state passes through the moment of fire and light…

And is flame not also the elusive and proud form of the most noble destruction? – What will never happen again, magnificently happens before our eyes! – What will never happen again, must happen as magnificently as possible! – As the voice sings wildly, as the flame sings madly between matter and ether – and from matter to ether rumbles and rushes furiously – is not the grand Dance, oh my friends, this deliverance from our body entirely possessed by the spirit of lies, and of music which is a lie, and drunk with the negation of null reality? – Look at that body, which leaps as flame replaces flame, look how it treads and tramples on what is true! How it furiously, joyously, destroys the very place where it is, and how it intoxicates itself with the excess of its changes!

But how it fights against the spirit! Can you not see that it wants with its soul for speed and variety? It is strangely jealous of this freedom and ubiquity which it thinks the mind possesses!...

Without doubt, the unique and perpetual object of the soul is that which does not exist : that which was, and that which is no longer ; – that which will be and is not yet ; – that which is possible, and impossible – what is the business of the soul, but never, *never*, what is!

And the body which is what is, it can no longer contain itself in the expanse! – Where to put itself? – Where to become? – This *One* wants to play as *All*. It wants to play at the universality of the soul! It wants to make up for its identity by the number of its acts! Being a thing, it bursts into events! – It gets carried away! – And like excited thought touches every substance, vibrates between time and instants, overcomes all differences ; and just as in our mind hypotheses are formed symmetrically, and as the possibilities fall into place and are counted, – this body exercises itself in all its parts, and combines with itself, gives itself form after form, and comes out of itself incessantly! Here it is at last in a state comparable to the flame, in the midst of the most active exchanges... We can no longer speak of "movement"... We can longer distinguish between its actions and its limbs...

That woman who was there is devoured by innumerable figures... That body, in its bursts of vigour, offers me an extreme thought : even as we ask of our soul things for which it was not made, and demand of it to enlighten us, so that it prophesises, that it foresees the future, imploring it even to discover God, – so the body which is there, wants to attain a complete self-possession, and a point of supernatural glory!... But it is the same for the body as for the soul, for which the God, and the wisdom, and the depth demanded of it, are and can only be moments, flashes, fragments of an alien time, desperate leaps out of its form...

Phaedrus

Look, just look!... She dances over there and gives to the eyes what here you are trying to tell us... She makes you see the moment... Oh through what jewels she passes!... She casts her gestures like sparkles!... She steals impossible attitudes from nature, under the very eye of Time!... Time lets itself be deceived... She crosses through the absurd with impunity... She is divine in the unstable, she is giving it to us as a gift!...

Eryximachus

The moment generates the form, and the form makes the moment visible.

Phaedrus

She flees her shadow up into the air!

Socrates

We only ever see her before she falls…

Eryximachus

She made her whole body as fluid, as well bound as an agile hand… My hand alone can imitate this possession and ease in all her body…

Socrates

Oh my friends, do you not feel intoxicated by jerks and jolts, and as if by repeated blows of more and more strength, little by little made to look like all those stamping dining guests, who can no longer keep their demons silent and hidden? I myself feel invaded by extraordinary forces… Or I feel that they come out from me, not knowing that I contained these virtues. In a world of sound, resonating and rebounding, this intense festival of the body before our souls offers light and joy… Everything is more solemn, everything is more light, everything is more lively, more strong ; everything is possible in another way ; everything can start again indefinitely… Nothing resists the alternation of the strong and the weak… Beat, beat!… Matter struck and beaten, colliding, in rhythm ; the earth well beaten ; skins and strings well stretched, well struck ; palms of hands, heels, striking well and beating time, forging joy and madness ; and all things in rhythmic delirium, reign.

But the growing and rebounding joy tends to overflow all measure, shakes the walls between human beings with a battering ram. Men and women in rhythm lead the song until tumult. Everyone beats and sings at once, and something grows and rises… I hear the din of all life's sparkling weapons!.. The cymbals crush any voice of secret thoughts in our ears. They are as loud as kisses from lips of bronze…

Eryximachus

Athikte nevertheless presents one final figure. Her whole body moves around on this big powerful toe.

Phaedrus

Her toe, which supports her entirely, rubs on the floor like her thumb on a drum. What attention there is in that toe ; what a will that stiffens it, and keeps it on that point!... But then she turns on herself...

Socrates

She turns round herself, – and then things eternally linked begin to separate. She turns and turns...

Eryximachus

It is truly like entering into another world...

Socrates

It is the ultimate attempt... She turns, and everything that is visible, detaches from her soul ; all the mud of her soul finally separated from what about it is purest ; men and things are going to form around her a shapeless, circular dreg…

You see… She turns… A body, by its simple force, and its act, is powerful enough to alter the nature of things more deeply than the mind in its speculations and dreams was ever able to.

Phaedrus

You would think that this could last forever.

Socrates

She could die, also…

Eryximachus

Sleep, perhaps, a magical sleep…

Socrates

She would rest motionless in the very centre of her movement. Isolated, alone, like the axis of the world…

Phaedrus

She turns, she turns… She falls!

Socrates

She has fallen!

Phaedrus

She is dead…

Socrates

She has exhausted her second wind, and the most hidden treasure in her frame!

Phaedrus

Gods! She might die… Eryximachus, go!…

Eryximachus

I do not have the habit of hurrying in such circumstances! If things are going to work out, the doctor should not interfere, and should arrive a very short time before the recovery, at the same pace as the Gods.

Socrates

It is necessary however to go see.

Phaedrus

How white she is!

Eryximachus

Allow rest to cure her of her movement.

Phaedrus

You think she is not dead?

Eryximachus

Look at this tiny breast that only wants to live. See how faintly it beats, suspended in time…

Phaedrus

I see it all too well.

Eryximachus

The bird flaps its wings a little, before it takes off again.

Socrates

She seems happy enough.

Phaedrus

What did she say?

Socrates

She said something for herself alone.

Eryximachus

She said : *How well I am!*

Phaedrus

This little pile of limbs and scarves is growing restless.

Eryximachus

Come, little child, let's open our eyes again. How do you feel now?

Athikte

I feel nothing. I am not dead. And yet, I am not alive!

Socrates

From where did you come back?

Athikte

Refuge, refuge, oh my refuge, oh whirlwind! – I was in you, oh movement, outside of all things…

www.ingramcontent.com/pod-product-compliance
Lightning Source LLC
Chambersburg PA
CBHW072106110526
44590CB00018B/3343